BATS

A WARD LOCK BOOK

First published in the UK 1996
by Ward Lock
Wellington House
125 Strand
LONDON
WC2R 0BB

A Cassell Imprint

Original title of the book in Spanish:
El Fascinante Mundo de Los Murciélagos

© Copyright Parramón Ediciones,
S.A. - World Rights
Published by Parramón Ediciones,
S.A., Barcelona, Spain

Author: Maria Ángels Julivert
Illustrator: Marcel Socías Studios

English translation © Copyright 1994
Barron's Educational Series, Inc.

Distributed in Australia
by Capricorn Link (Australia) Pty Ltd
2/13 Carrington Road, Castle Hill NSW 2154

A British Library Cataloguing in Publication Data block for
this book may be obtained from the British Library.

ISBN Hardback 0 7063 7545 9
       Paperback 0 7063 7551 3
Printed and bound in Spain

THE FASCINATING WORLD OF...

BATS

by
Maria Ángels Julivert

Illustrations by Marcel Socías Studios

WARD LOCK

PECULIAR MAMMALS

Bats belong to the order *Chiroptera,* which means "with wings on their hands." Although sometimes they appear strange to us, and often frightening, they are exceptional mammals.

Their most surprising characteristics are their ability to fly and their use of **echolocation** (see page 8).

Like all mammals, bats have body hair, although it is short. They undergo two teethings, milk teeth and final teeth. The female has mammary glands to suckle her young.

Bats' forelimbs are highly modified to support their wings, which are hairless. The thumb is the only free finger, and is armed with a claw that the bat uses for gripping, climbing, and moving when it is not in the air. The lower limbs are less developed; each have five toes equipped with strong claws that the bat uses to hang upside down.

Another strange aspect of bats is the knee, which bends backwards instead of forwards. On the ankle bats have a spur, called a **calcar** or heel.

No other mammal has adapted itself as well as chiropterans to life in the air, although some mammals, like the "flying" squirrel, glide from tree to tree.

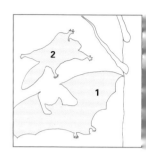

Right: Bats are the only mammals adapted for true flight. Their forelimbs have been transformed into wings (1).
Some rodents, like the "flying" squirrel (2), can glide long distances from one tree to another.

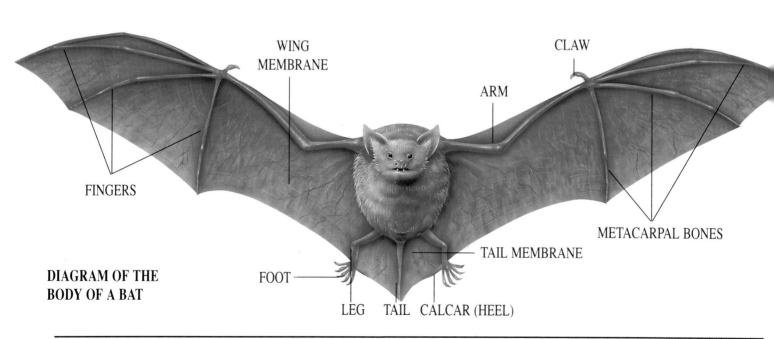

WING MEMBRANE

CLAW

ARM

FINGERS

METACARPAL BONES

TAIL MEMBRANE

DIAGRAM OF THE BODY OF A BAT

FOOT

LEG   TAIL   CALCAR (HEEL)

SKILFUL FLIERS

Bats, like birds, are adapted to life in the air. However, they do not fly as well as birds, and their wings are very different.

A bat's wings are composed of a double layer of skin, containing numerous blood vessels, connective tissue fibres, and nerves. This fine membrane, called the **patagium,** stretches across both sides of the body and is supported by the fingers and the upper and lower limbs. The finger bones, except for the thumb, are very long and resemble the spokes of an umbrella.

The **patagium** is almost entirely hairless. It is divided into three parts: **propatagium,** the membrane in front of the forearms; **plagiopatagium,** the main wing membrane, and **uropatagium,** or tail membrane, although this last is not present in some species. Some bats have short, wide wings and do not fly very fast but can perform sudden turns in the air quickly and easily. Other bats have long, narrow wings and can fly high and fast but cannot manoeuvre as well. When they are not flying, they hang upside down, holding on with their strong claws, and with their wings folded. Some species wrap their wings around their bodies like cloaks, while others fold them at their sides.

When they take off, they let go and open their wings.

TYPES OF WINGS

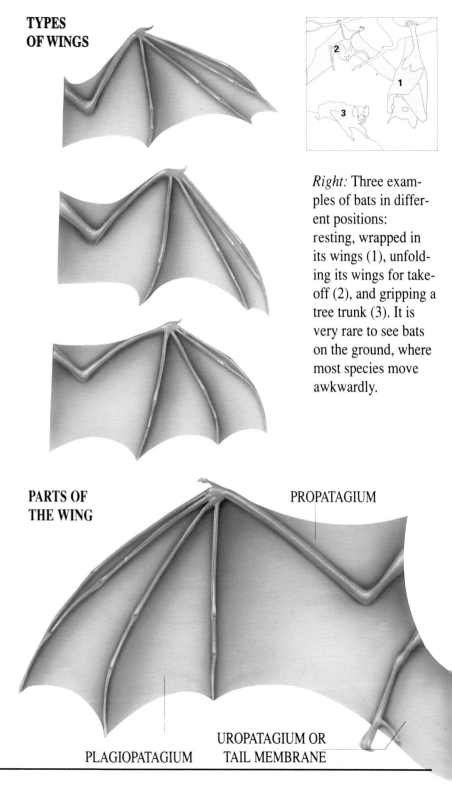

Right: Three examples of bats in different positions: resting, wrapped in its wings (1), unfolding its wings for take-off (2), and gripping a tree trunk (3). It is very rare to see bats on the ground, where most species move awkwardly.

PARTS OF THE WING

PROPATAGIUM

PLAGIOPATAGIUM

UROPATAGIUM OR TAIL MEMBRANE

MANOEUVRING IN THE DARK

Bats are nocturnal animals; the majority do not have very good eyesight. However, they have developed extraordinary hearing.

These mammals have evolved an ingenious means of locating their prey and of finding their way in the dark, avoiding any objects in their way. While they fly, they constantly emit sounds, which rebound off other objects. The resulting echo is picked up by the bat, telling it the exact location of any obstacles ahead (distance, direction, etc). This phenomenon is known as **echolocation.**

The signals the bat emits are high frequency sounds that cannot be detected by humans. This system of radar is not the same in all **species.** Many types of bats emit sounds through the mouth. They sometimes have a lobe of skin in the ears, called a **tragus,** which helps their aural perception. Still other species emit screeches via the nose.

Megachiroptera, except for one genus, do not use echolocation. Sight and smell are more important to them.

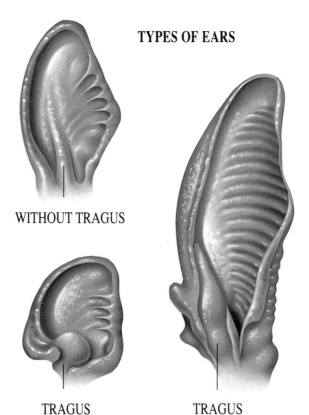

TYPES OF EARS

WITHOUT TRAGUS

TRAGUS

TRAGUS

NOSE OF A HORSESHOE BAT

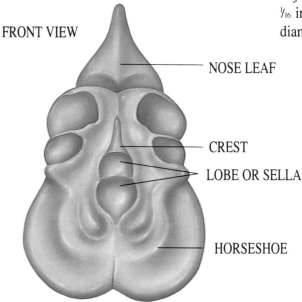

FRONT VIEW

NOSE LEAF

CREST

LOBE OR SELLA

HORSESHOE

Right: The horseshoe bat belongs to a species that emits squeaks through its nose. It has folds of skin around the nose that help focus the sound, although it gives the bat a rather grotesque appearance.

Other species emit sounds through the mouth. The sounds rebound from objects and are picked up by the mammal's acute hearing.

Using echolocation, bats can detect incredibly small objects, of less than $\frac{1}{16}$ inch (1 mm) in diameter.

NURSERY COLONIES

Most bats reproduce once a year. They usually give birth to one or two young at a time, although some bats can have up to three.

The young are born completely formed, without hair, and with closed eyes. They are carried by clinging tightly to the mother's breast.

In some species, after mating takes place, usually in autumn, the male's sperm are stored in the female's body until the spring, when **fertilisation** takes place. In other species, fertilisation occurs immediately after mating, but the development of the embryo is delayed until conditions are favourable. In some bat species the females with young separate from the males. Others stay together and form large nursery colonies. While the females go to hunt for food, the young remain in the roost, awaiting their return. When the mothers come back, they locate their young by their cries and feed them.

The females of some species always carry their young with them, even during their nocturnal flights in search of food.

The young bats stay with their mothers until they have learned to fly and are able to care for themselves.

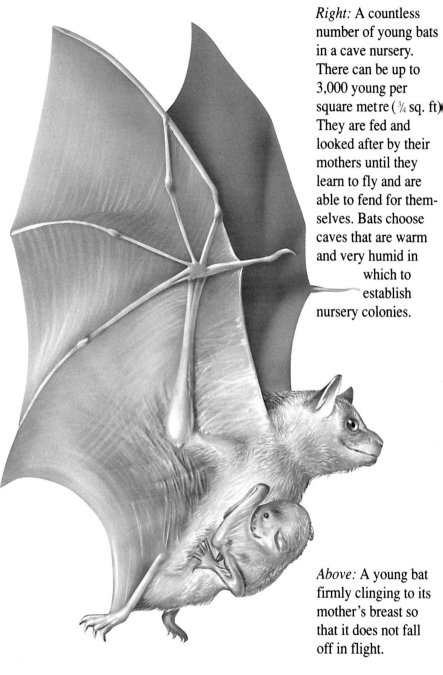

Right: A countless number of young bats in a cave nursery. There can be up to 3,000 young per square metre (¾ sq. ft) They are fed and looked after by their mothers until they learn to fly and are able to fend for themselves. Bats choose caves that are warm and very humid in which to establish nursery colonies.

Above: A young bat firmly clinging to its mother's breast so that it does not fall off in flight.

A VARIED DIET

The diet of bats is very varied. Most are **insectivores.** That is to say, they eat insects that they catch in flight, among vegetation, or on the ground. Some also eat spiders and other small **invertebrates.**

They are skilful fliers and can perform abrupt turns in the air, or dive suddenly. They catch insects in their mouths or hold them in their tail **membranes,** which they use like a net.

There are also **carnivorous** bats, which hunt small mammals, birds, lizards, and even frogs. Some species also catch fish.

Other bats prefer to feed on fruit, which they grip with their claws and press against their chests to drink the juice.

There are sweet-toothed bats whose diet consists of nectar and pollen from flowers, although they will also eat any insects they come across. They have an extended muzzle and a long, bristly tongue.

A curious case are vampire bats, which only feed on blood that they lap from other mammals, especially cattle and horses.

Most bats use **echolocation** to find their prey. However, species that feed on fruit, pollen, and nectar rely on their excellent sight and sense of smell.

Right: An insectivorous bat and a carnivorous bat hunting for food. From top to bottom, the jaw bone of an insectivore, a vampire bat, a nectar feeder, an omnivore, a fruit eater, and a carnivore.

NECTAR FEEDER

CARNIVORE

VAMPIRE

FISH EATER

INSECTIVORE

FRUIT EATER

WINTER LETHARGY

Most bats that live in cold or temperate climates **hibernate** during the winter months.

At this time of year temperatures fall a great deal and food becomes scarce. Bats do not have efficient **thermoregulation.** For this reason they enter a period of torpor or **lethargy.** During this period, their metabolism slows down and they nourish themselves from the reserves of fat that they have acquired during the **autumn.**

Tropical species, on the other hand, do not need to hibernate.

There is a difference between the torpor of **hibernation** and the drowsiness they experience during daily periods of rest.

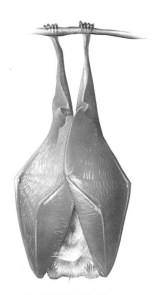

A BAT WRAPPED IN ITS PATAGIUM OR WING MEMBRANE

PROTECTION FROM THE COLD

COVERED IN DEW

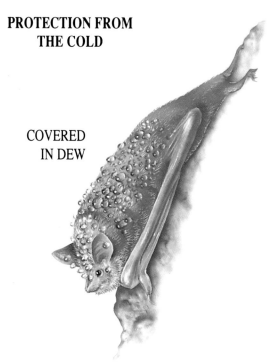

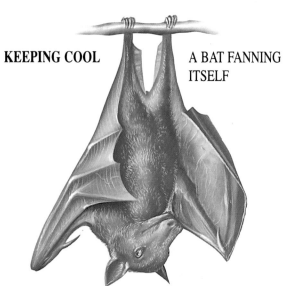

KEEPING COOL

A BAT FANNING ITSELF

When they rest their body temperature falls but not to the same levels as when they are hibernating.

Most bats hibernate in large groups, roosting in caves and grottos. They normally choose enclosed sites where humidity is high in order to avoid dehydration. From time to time they wake up to move, change place, or drink. Some bats migrate at certain times of the year, sometimes covering large distances of up to hundreds of miles. Others move much shorter distances.

There are also bats that stay in the same area throughout their entire lives and only move to change their roost.

Right: In temperate regions when winter comes, insectivorous bats go on migrations to warmer areas, just like birds.

It is not known how bats orientate themselves during migration, nor how they are capable of returning to the place from which they set off. There remain many mysteries about bats to be uncovered.

DIFFERENT DWELLINGS

Bats can be found in many different **habitats.** They live in jungles, arid regions, fields, gardens, and even in inhabited areas.

They are nocturnal animals and during the day they roost in very varied places. They hang from rocky walls and overhangs, or they hide in crevices. They can also be found in the depths of forests, hanging from the branches of trees. They are seen in abandoned houses and barns, clinging to beams, walls, and hanging under roofs. Other bats prefer hollow trees and many take refuge in caves and grottos.

An interesting case are certain tropical bats that nibble the large leaves of palm trees to make a kind of tent under which they find shelter.

Most bats live in groups, some large, others small. Only a few species are solitary. Some bat colonies are composed of thousands, and sometimes millions, of bats.

The males and the females of some species live separately and only come together to mate. Others form mixed colonies and live together for most of the year, except when the females separate themselves to give birth.

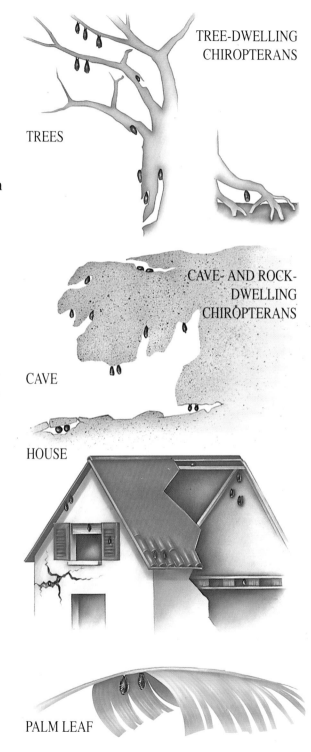

TREE-DWELLING CHIROPTERANS

TREES

CAVE- AND ROCK-DWELLING CHIROPTERANS

CAVE

HOUSE

PALM LEAF

Right: These bats chew through the stems and veins of leaves to fold them down and be protected from sun, wind, rain, and predators. The small holes that are left where they have chewed are used for holding on.

Left: Diagrams showing the different types of daily roost. Bats that live in trees are called tree-dwelling chiropterans and those that live in caves are called cave- and rock-dwelling chiropterans.

HUGE VARIETY OF SPECIES

Among mammals, the order *Chiroptera* is one of the most numerous, second only to rodents. Over 900 species of bats have been identified, each of different size, appearance, and habits.

Sometimes it is difficult to distinguish one from another, but there are many details that can help to identify them: wings, ears, teeth (which indicate the diet), muzzle, and tail (which can be long or short, joined to the tail **membrane** or free, and sometimes not present at all). Bats vary greatly in size. The smallest measure only 6 inches (15 cm.) across, the largest up to 80 inches (2 metres).

Bats can be found in all parts of the world except in cold regions like Antarctica.

They are divided into two large groups: **megachiroptera** and **microchiroptera,** which are more numerous. The former have large eyes and ears, an extended muzzle, and both the thumb and the second finger have a claw. They do not have protuberant noses nor tragi in the ears. They are generally large and can be found in Asia, Africa, and Australia. **Microchiroptera** have smaller eyes and only have one claw, which is on the thumb. Many have tragi in the ears and some have strange-looking folds of skin on the nose. They can be found on almost every continent except Antarctica.

Right: Chiroptera of different species. A Mexican free-tailed bat hanging from a branch (1). A greater horseshoe bat wrapped in its wing membrane (2). A mouse-tailed bat in flight (3). A parti-coloured bat descending a tree trunk (4).

TYPES OF TAILS

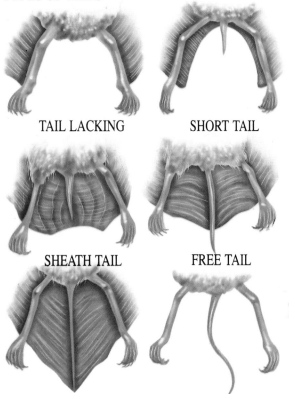

TAIL LACKING

SHORT TAIL

SHEATH TAIL

FREE TAIL

FULL MEMBRANE

MOUSE TAIL

BATS' HEADS

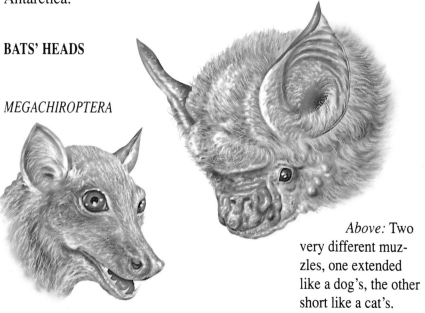

MEGACHIROPTERA

MICROCHIROPTERA

Above: Two very different muzzles, one extended like a dog's, the other short like a cat's.

FLYING FOXES

Megachiroptera, or flying foxes, have an enlarged muzzle, and a head that resembles a fox's head, giving them their name.

They live in tropical and subtropical areas of Asia, Africa, and Australia. This group includes the largest bats, with wingspans of over 39 inches (1 metre) and weighing more than 2 pounds (1 kilo). It also includes small bats with a wingspan of 12 inches (30 cm.) and weighing ¹/₂ ounce (15 grams).

Flying foxes have a highly developed sense of smell and acute vision, which they use to orientate themselves and to find food. Only bats of the genus *Rousettus* use **echolocation.** They produce sounds by clicking their tongue, unlike **Microchiroptera,** which make sounds from the larynx. Flying foxes eat fruit, flowers, **nectar,** and, in some cases, pollen. They frequently cover large distances in their search for food. Fruit-eating species, like the Indian flying fox, are generally very large.

The species whose diet is mostly pollen are small and have a pointed muzzle and a long, extendible tongue with small bristles on the tip to gather the pollen from flowers.

THE TONGUE OF A *MEGACHIROPTERA* SPECIMEN FEEDING ON POLLEN

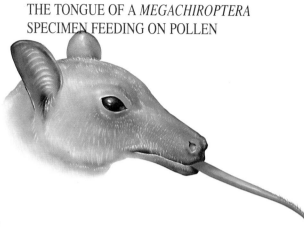

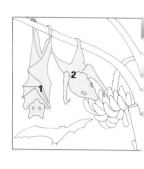

FILIFORM PAPILLAE

DETAIL OF THE TONGUE

Right: A flying fox resting (1). A fruit-eating bat feeding on bananas (2). With the claws of its forefinger and thumb and its feet, it clings to the fruit and laps its juice.

A HAMMER-HEAD BAT

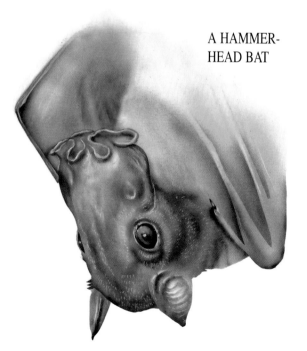

Left: The male hammer-head bat is bigger than the female. To attract the female during courtship, the male lets out loud screeches, while shaking his wings.

SMALL BATS

Microchiroptera, called **insectivorous** bats (although not all of them are insectivorous) are found on almost every continent. They are more numerous, include a great number of species, and are very varied in appearance.

The smallest known bat belongs to this group, as does the vampire bat, the common pipistrelle and the horseshoe bat. Their colouring is generally subdued and is fairly uniform in appearance, with tones ranging from black or chestnut to reddish brown. Few bats are hairless, and most are covered in fur except for some parts of the head, wing, tail, and neck. The ears of some *Microchiroptera* are surprisingly large, like the long-eared bat. Some have folds on the nose, like the horseshoe bat.

Bats leave their roosts at nightfall in search of food. Most are **insectivores;** their preferred prey is moths, mosquitoes, and beetles.

Carnivorous species catch frogs, birds, and even small mammals such as mice. Some species feed on pollen. Most *Microchiroptera* are gregarious and group together to create colonies.

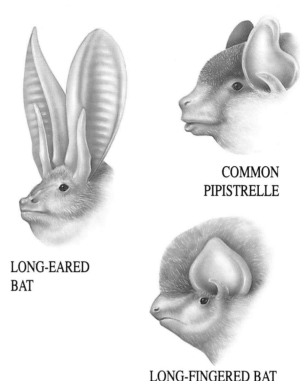

LONG-EARED BAT

COMMON PIPISTRELLE

LONG-FINGERED BAT

Right: An insect-eating bat entering a cave with its favourite food.

Below: Map of distribution of different bat species in the world.

Colonies of Brazilian or Mexican free-tailed bats in New Mexico can total millions of individual animals.

BRAZILIAN OR MEXICAN FREE-TAILED BAT

VAMPIRE BAT

HORSESHOE BAT

COMMON PIPISTRELLE

LONG-FINGERED BAT

HAIRLESS BAT

VAMPIRES

Without a doubt the bats that inspire the most fear and that have the worst reputation are vampire bats. They have inspired all kinds of tales and legends due to their strange diet. They feed exclusively on the blood of mammals and birds, above all domestic animals, although they can also attack humans.

There are only three **species** of **sanguivore** (blood-eating) bats, all living in tropical areas of America.

The best known is the common vampire bat. Its favourite prey is mammals, particularly cattle and horses. It hunts at night, and flies low, skimming the ground. When it locates its victim, it lands and approaches silently. Sometimes it even climbs on top of its prey, searching for a part of the body without much hair (ears, snout, feet) in which to insert its two large, razor-sharp incisors. It makes a small cut and licks the wound. The animal does not wake up because the bite is hardly noticeable.

Because of an anticoagulant in the bat's saliva, the blood continues to flow from the open wound for a long time. When it has satisfied its hunger, the bat returns to its roost: a cave, a crevice, or a hole in a tree.

The other two species are less common and prefer to attack birds.

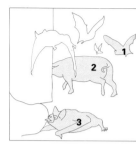

Right: Blood-eating bats (1), flying above the next victim, a pig (2). Another vampire bat (3) lapping the blood from the snout of a sleeping pig.

Above: The two razor-sharp upper incisors of the common vampire bat, with which it can make a cut in its victim unnoticed.

Below: The common vampire bat is extremely agile and can jump on four legs like a frog, or walk like a monkey.

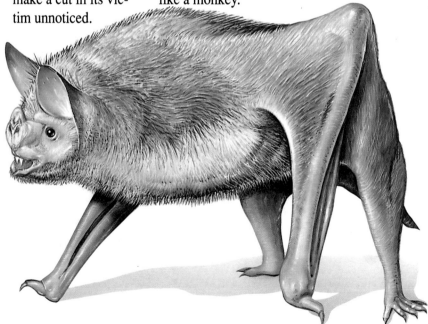

SKILFUL AT FISHING

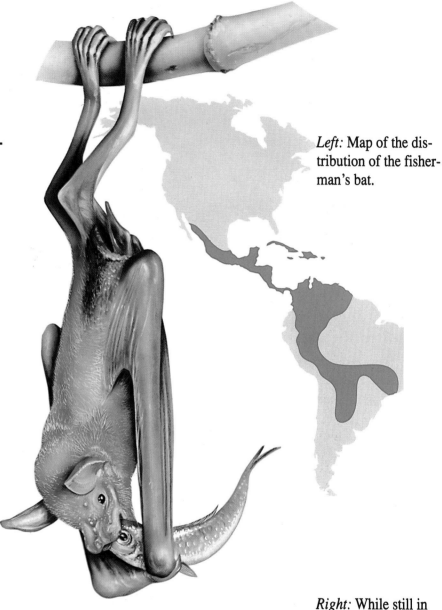

The favourite food of some **chiropterans** is fish. The fisherman's bat lives in tropical forests, from Mexico to Argentina. Its body is covered in short hair, orange coloured on the male and chestnut on the female. It is perfectly adapted for this type of diet. Its hind legs are long and muscular and are equipped with powerful talons, which it uses to catch elusive prey.

Fisherman's bats always live close to water—rivers, lakes, or lagoons—where they find their main source of food.

Like most bats, the fisherman's bat rests in groups during the day, hanging upside down among trees, in caves, or in crevices of rocks.

At nightfall the bat goes to hunt, almost always alone. It flies slowly over the surface of the water in search of fish, and can detect the slightest ripple or splash of water. Then it swiftly dips its claws below the surface and grabs its prey, without getting its wings wet, immediately putting the animal between its jaws. Sometimes it takes the fish back to its shelter to eat it.

Left: Map of the distribution of the fisherman's bat.

Right: While still in flight these bats can fish, grabbing their prey with the talons of their hind feet. They then carry them away or eat them in flight.

Above: Its claws are remarkably long and powerful. On its back there are large areas without hair.

OF BATS AND MEN

Because of their bizarre appearance and their nocturnal customs, bats have inspired innumerable horror stories. Nevertheless, most bats are harmless.

In some regions, large **frugivore** (fruit-eating) bats can cause damage to plantations if they gather in large numbers. However, many bats are beneficial to humans and their crops.

Bats that feed on fruit, flowers, and pollen help the dissemination of seeds and the **pollination** of many plants.

Insectivore (insect-eating) bats eliminate large numbers of insects, some of which can destroy crops.

The **guano** that bats produce is used as an excellent fertiliser. Natives of Africa, India, and Australia catch flying foxes for their meat, which is much appreciated. But indiscriminate hunting, the use of insecticides, and the destruction of their habitats and roosts have put these interesting mammals in danger. Many species are already extinct.

THE FOOD CHAIN

HAWK

INSECT

BAT

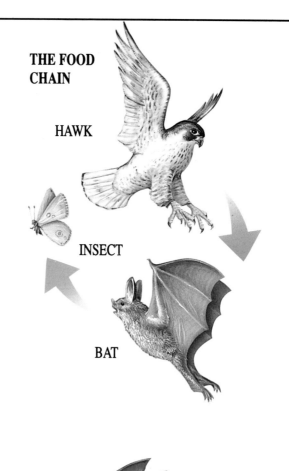

Right: These bats have a long, extendible tongue that allows them to lap up nectar from flowers. They aid the pollination of flowers because they transport pollen from one flower to another.

Left: A sequence in the food chain. The bird of prey pursues the bat that in turn pursues the insect.

POLLINATION HELPED BY BATS

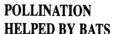

Glossary

colony: A group of animals of the same species that live together.

echolocation: The system of acoustic detection that allows bats and other mammals to orientate themselves by emitting ultrasounds that bounce off other objects.

fertilisation: The joining together of male and female cells to create a new being.

frugivore: An animal that feeds on fruit.

guano: The excrement of certain animals used as fertiliser, particularly when it has decomposed.

habitat: Part of the physical surroundings where an animal lives.

hibernation: The state of inactivity that some animals undergo in winter to survive adverse conditions. During this period, body temperature falls and there is a general decrease in metabolism.

insectivore: An animal that feeds on insects.

invertebrates: The group of animals that lack a vertebral column.

Megachiroptera: Megabats. A sub-order of mammals of the order *Chiroptera,* which includes larger bats. They have large eyes and a muzzle like a fox. Most are fruit eaters.

Microchiroptera: Microbats. A sub-order of mammals of the order *Chiroptera,* which includes, among others, insectivorous bats. They are usually small or medium-sized.

migration: Periodic or occasional movement from one place to another, for climatic, reproductive, or feeding reasons.

nectar: The sweet liquid produced by many flowers.

patagium: The membrane of skin that is attached to the fingers, legs, and tails of bats and that allows them to fly.

pollination: The transfer of pollen from the stamen of one flower to the female part of another, thus fertilising the plant.

sanguivore: An animal that feeds on blood, like the vampire bat.

species: A group of animals or plants that have a series of characteristics in common, by which they resemble each other and are distinguishable from other species.

thermoregulation: The mechanism by which mammals try to maintain a constant body temperature when exposed to variations in the ambient temperature.

torpor: The state of drowsiness into which some animals sink during certain times of the year.

tragus: A prominence at the entrance of the external ear situated in front of the aural orifice. It is present in some bats.

ultrasound: A sound whose wave frequency is above the limit audible to the human ear.

vertebrates: The group of animals that have a skeleton with a vertebral column. Included in this group are fish, amphibians, reptiles, birds, and mammals.

INDEX

This book is due for return on or before the last date shown below.